Contents

Some words are shown in bold, **like this**. You can find out what they mean by looking in the Glossary.

Made in Mainz

Man with a mission

Johannes Gutenberg (about 1398–1468) spent his life on a great project, only to see his dream fulfilled by his own business partner, rather than himself. Before Gutenberg's breakthrough, books were copied slowly, by hand. This made them incredibly expensive. Before Gutenberg, Europeans used carved wooden blocks to print playing-cards or souvenir pictures of saints. They used presses to crush grapes for their juice. Gutenberg combined these basic processes, adding further ideas to create a whole new printing technology. He aimed to produce whole books, printed from separate pieces of metal **type** which, unlike carved blocks, could be broken down and used again.

A replica of Gutenberg's printing-press is on display in his original workshop in Mainz, Germany.

Technical problems

Gutenberg was born in Mainz, Germany, and trained as a goldsmith. He became very skilled in working metal. He invented an adjustable mould so that he could **cast** uniform pieces of metal type – representing different letters of the alphabet – quickly and in large numbers. He perfected an **alloy** of tin, lead and **antimony** which melted easily, flowed evenly and cooled quickly. He designed an adjustable frame to hold separate letters as lines of print that would stay straight under pressure. He improved traditional presses to apply pressure evenly across paper and he developed a new kind of oil-based ink.

The Printing Press

A Breakthrough in Communication

RICHARD TAMES

Heinemann
LIBRARY

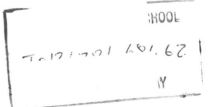

www.heinemann.co.uk
Visit our website to find out more information about **Heinemann Library** books.

To order:
 Phone 44 (0) 1865 888066
 Send a fax to 44 (0) 1865 314091
Visit the Heinemann Bookshop at www.heinemann.co.uk to browse our catalogue and order online.

First published in Great Britain by Heinemann Library,
Halley Court, Jordan Hill, Oxford OX2 8EJ,
a division of Reed Educational and Professional Publishing Ltd.
Heinemann is a registered trademark of Reed Educational & Professional Publishing Ltd.

OXFORD MELBOURNE AUCKLAND
JOHANNESBURG BLANTYRE GABORONE
IBADAN PORTSMOUTH NH (USA) CHICAGO

Designed by Robert Sydenham, Ambassador Design Ltd, Bristol.
Originated by Ambassador Litho, Bristol.
Printed by Wing King Tong Hong Kong

ISBN 0 431 06921 2 (hardback)   ISBN 0 431 06928 X (paperback)
05 04 03 02 01   05 04 03 02 01
10 9 8 7 6 5 4 3 2   10 9 8 7 6 5 4 3 2 1

British Library Cataloguing in Publication Data
Tames, Richard 1946–
Printing-press: a breakthrough in communication. – (Turning poi
1.Printing-press – Juvenile literature
2.Printing-press – History literature
1.Title
681.6'2

Acknowledgements
The Publishers would like to thank the following for permission to reproduce photographs:
Bridgeman: p. 9,(British Library) p. 6, (Christie's) p. 5, (The Stapleton Collection) p. 11, (Trinity College) p. 8; Corbis: pp. 18, 21, 28, (Michael Maslan) p. 14, (Underwood & Underwood) p. 4; Mary Evans Picture Library: pp. 7, 12; National Maritime Museum: p. 15; Tames, Richard: pp. 19, 22, 23, 26; The British Library: pp. 10, 20; University of Reading Library: pp. 16, 17; Victoria and Albert Museum: p. 13.

Cover photograph reproduced with permission of Corbis (Bettmann).

Our thanks to Christopher Gibb for his help in the preparation of this book.

Every effort has been made to contact copyright holders of any material reproduced in this book. Any omissions will be rectified in subsequent printings if notice is given to the Publisher.

Business problems

Around 1450 Gutenberg went into partnership with a lawyer, John Fust, who loaned him money for a printing business. In 1453 he began working on a three-volume Bible. This progressed very slowly and the partnership with Fust broke down in 1455. Because Gutenberg could not pay back the money to Fust, he had to surrender the press. Fust and his son-in-law Peter Schoffer, Gutenberg's assistant, actually finished the first printed Bible, but it is still known as Gutenberg's Bible.

Print against pen

One single hand-copied Bible would take a **scribe** about four years to finish. Twenty men produced 450 Gutenberg Bibles in one year. Therefore, each one was produced ninety times faster and cost only one tenth as much as a hand-copied version. Printing meant books were no longer only for the rich, but were for anyone who was **literate.** Instead of relying on a priest or scribe to tell them what a book said, people could read it for themselves. New ideas and new information meant new challenges to old ideas and the people who held on to them.

A page from the Gutenberg Bible of about 1450–55, set with 42 lines per column – the margin decorations were added by hand.

Asian advances

Sacred signs

Printing from carved wooden blocks, to reproduce religious writings and images, was being used in China, Korea and Japan by the 8th century AD. Rulers ordered mass production of these to bring their people good fortune and gain favour for themselves. Japan's Empress Koken (718–70) had a million charms printed to ward off smallpox – but died as the project was completed, probably of smallpox! In 983 the Chinese printed the Buddhist **scriptures** in 5048 separate volumes, totalling 130,000 pages, each page printed from a separately carved block.

A problem of language

In the 11th century, Korean and Chinese printers experimented with printing from single pieces of **type** put together in different combinations. In theory, their success was a big step forward, because block-printing could only produce the same whole page over and over again.

The *Diamond Sutra*, a Buddhist scripture, is one of the oldest complete printed books, with its known date of AD 868.

Fabrication du papier en Chine. — D'après les dessins de M. Marchal.

In practice, however, it did not help much, because the Chinese, Japanese and Korean alphabets were made up not of just a few letters, but of thousands of characters, each standing for a thing or an idea. To choose and put together a page from a huge store of characters, and then sort them out and put them back again, took a long time. In fact, it took so long that block-printing was not usually much slower – especially as they wanted to print the same religious books over and over again, rather than producing new ones. So this breakthrough came to nothing.

This 19th-century print shows people trimming and soaking bamboo to make paper in China.

PAPER

Paper was being used in China by AD 105. It was originally made from the inner bark of mulberry trees, soaked in water to make a pulp, which was pressed into sheets and dried. Later old rags, rope and even fishing nets were used. Coarser papers, made from straw or wood, were also manufactured, not for writing but for lanterns or fans or wrapping. Chinese prisoners captured in Central Asia had brought the secret of paper-making to the Arab world by 795. It reached Spain by the twelfth century and then Italy and England by the fourteenth century. Paper was less beautiful than **parchment,** which was made of animal skin. It did not last nearly as long but was much, much cheaper.

7

Scribes and scriptures

A little learning

Roman rule ended in western Europe in the 5th century AD. Towns and trade shrank. Almost the only **literate** people left were Christian priests, trained in **monasteries.** Each large monastery had a **scriptorium** where books were copied out by hand and novices were taught to read and write. They still used Latin, the language of the Romans, for writing and worship.

Scribes usually wrote with goose-feather **quills** and ink made from soot and oil. They could copy up to four pages a day. They wrote on **parchment** made from the scraped skins of calves, sheep or goats. A book of 350 pages would take the skins of 200 calves. Most monastery libraries had only a few dozen books, which they loaned to each other so they could all make their own copies.

Kings and nobles relied on scribes to keep records and accounts for them, write letters and draw up **charters** and **treaties.** Latin was also used for all these purposes throughout Europe, whatever language was spoken locally.

Eadwine, a Canterbury monk, drew this picture of himself working on a book of Psalms in about 1150.

English achievements

In England, King Alfred (849–899) had books translated from Latin and copied by hand, in English, so more people could read them. He also ordered a **chronicle** of important events to be kept in English. England also produced one of the greatest books of the Middle Ages. In 1086 William I (about 1027–87) ordered a complete survey of the kingdom. It was compiled by monks who usually spoke French, asked questions in English and wrote in Latin. The people called the completed survey the *Domesday Book* because it reminded them of God calling everyone to account on the Day of Judgement.

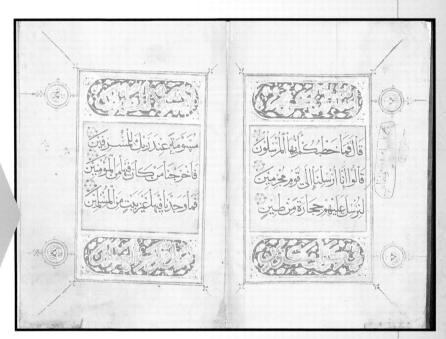

This Qur'an was handwritten in Turkey in the 14th century.

SACRED WORDS

Throughout the Middle Ages Christians and Muslims were often at war. But both religions agreed the most important books were those recording the words of God – the Bible and the Qur'an. Bibles and Qur'ans were written in beautiful **calligraphy** and bound in splendid covers, often decorated with gold or jewels.

In 698 Eadfrith, Bishop of Lindisfarne, an island off the English coast, began copying out the four Gospels in Latin. It took him three years. Around 950 Aeldred, a monk, wrote an Anglo-Saxon translation between the lines of Eadfrith's text – the first Christian **scripture** in English.

Master Caxton's hobby

A second career

William Caxton (about 1422–91) was an English merchant who lived in Bruges in Flanders (now part of Belgium) and in Westminster, in London. Printing presses – based on Gutenberg's ideas – had been set up in both cities. In his spare time Caxton translated stories from French into English. He became interested in having them printed so that more of his friends could read them.

The first book he had printed, which he had himself translated, was about the history of ancient Troy. He also printed one about chess. Retiring from business in 1476, Caxton brought a press back to England, setting it up in Westminster. Over the next fifteen years he printed about a hundred different books, including the poems of Geoffrey Chaucer and the stories of King Arthur and the Knights of the Round Table.

This illustrated page is from Chaucer's *Canterbury Tales*, printed by Caxton in 1483.

Which English?

Caxton had to decide what sort of English to print. There was no standard form. The words people used and the way they said them differed widely from region to region. Caxton himself wrote how a storm once forced two London merchants to stop in Kent only a few dozen miles down river. When one asked a local farmer's wife to sell them eggs to eat, she said that she didn't understand him because she could not speak French. He was cross because he did not speak French either! In Kent eggs were called eyren, which sounds very like their modern German name.

IMPRESSIO LIBRORVM.

Poteſt vt vna vox capi aure plurima: *Linunt ita vna ſcripta mille paginas.*

A print shop in Germany in the 1500s.

Caxton also noted that *'certaynly our langage now used varyeth ferre from that which was used and spoken when I was borne'*. When he was printing his books, Caxton used the English of London and the south-east. Over time, printing gradually fixed the spelling of words and made that particular dialect the basis of 'standard English' as used by educated people, and on public occasions.

WHERE TO DO BUSINESS?

Caxton chose Westminster Abbey to site his press and bookshop because he thought its monks and visitors would be good customers. When he died he left his business to his assistant, Wynkyn de Worde (died 1535), who moved it to Fleet Street in the City of London. He thought the rich merchants and nobles living there would be even better customers. For the next five centuries Fleet Street and the area around St Paul's Cathedral would be the home of English printing and publishing.

Bibles and beliefs

Luther

Throughout the Middle Ages, Christians in western Europe obeyed the Roman Catholic Church, headed by the pope. Its teachings were based on the Bible but included many extra rules made by popes and councils of priests. Protestantism was a protest movement, led by a German priest, Martin Luther (1483–1546). He

believed the Church was more concerned with wealth than saving souls. Luther argued that the Bible alone supplied correct Christian beliefs. This became the core Protestant idea. Luther translated the Bible from Latin into German so that more people could read it for themselves.

Reformation

A century earlier, the Bohemian Jan Hus (1370–1415) and Englishman John Wycliffe (about 1330–84) had held the same ideas as Luther, but they failed to start mass movements. Printing made all the difference. The cheap Bibles first printed in Germany – as a result of Gutenberg's work – spread Protestantism into neighbouring Switzerland, France, Holland and Britain. This became known as the Reformation because Protestants set up separate – Reformed – Churches. They refused to obey the pope and followed new ways of worshipping, based on the Bible. Protestant worship stressed study of the Bible, with preachers explaining its meaning in **sermons.**

William Tyndale (1494–1536) translated the New Testament into English. He knew Luther and Gutenberg's assistant, Schoeffer. Tyndale was burned at the stake in 1536 for **heresy**.

Books and belief

Most people were too poor to own books, but if a Protestant family did have one it was a Bible. It was certainly the book everybody, **literate** or not, knew best and it affected the language people used, from everyday speech to poetry. Luther's Bible set the standard for how German should be written. In Wales, from the 1540s onwards, English was the language of government and law. The appearance of a Welsh Bible in 1588 kept Welsh alive as the language of religion.

For two centuries after Luther, Europe was torn by religious wars – between Catholics and Protestants and between different Protestants. One of the main reasons English people began to emigrate to America was so that they would be free to worship in their own way.

This picture from a 19th-century edition of Foxe's *Book of Martyrs* shows two Protestant bishops, Latimer and Ridley, being burned at Oxford in 1555, during the reign of the Catholic Queen Mary I.

BEST-SELLERS

Religion was the main subject of the most famous books printed in this period. After the Bible, the most popular book in England at the time was Foxe's *Book of Martyrs* (first published in 1554), about Protestants who had died for their beliefs. John Milton's long poem *Paradise Lost* explains how Satan, originally an angel, was thrown out of Heaven. John Bunyan's *The Pilgrim's Progress* told how its hero, Christian, came through many dangers and evils to reach Heaven at last.

Printing the world

Secret knowledge

Printing made books cheaper and more plentiful. But this did not mean the information in them was more accurate. This was even more true of maps. Before printing was developed, maps were drawn by hand. This made it easier to control how many were produced and circulated. Trading countries such as Portugal and the Netherlands grew rich bringing spices from Asia. They tried to keep knowledge about the sea-routes to Asia to themselves. After Englishman Francis Drake sailed right round the world (1577–80) his **logbook** was kept top secret and no mention of his adventure appeared in print for over ten years. Long after printing developed, seamen continued to rely on hand-drawn maps as being more reliable, easier to keep up-dated – and secret.

Profit before truth

Early printed maps were produced using engraved blocks of wood. After about 1550 the wooden blocks were replaced by copper printing plates. These were very expensive to prepare. Printers often refused to throw them away, even after new geographical discoveries. Sometimes they just kept printing the same old maps. Sometimes they even sold them alongside newer ones which contradicted them. A Portuguese ship sailed round Africa into the Indian Ocean in 1497, but maps ignoring this sea route to India were still being sold in 1570.

This 19th-century map shows how the Flemish map-maker Geradus Mercator (1512–94) changed our way of looking at the world, by treating it as an exploded globe.

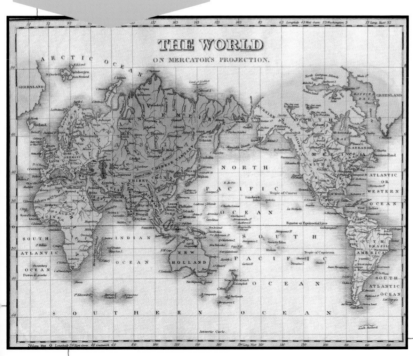

THE WORLD
ON MERCATOR'S PROJECTION.

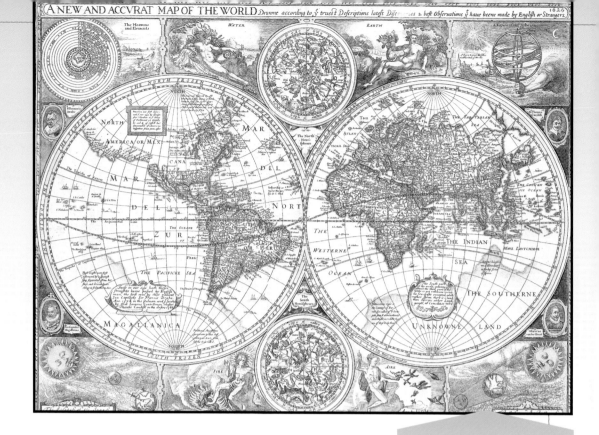

An English world map, first drawn in around 1610, pays tribute to Drake and other explorers.

Naming America

Italian-born Amerigo Vespucci (1451–1512) sold supplies to Christopher Columbus before himself voyaging to explore the coast of South America and writing a private letter in Italian describing his travels. This was later printed in Latin.

In 1507 Martin Waldseemüller (1470–1518), a German amateur printer, published a description of the world, including a large map printed from twelve wooden blocks, which drew on the Latin version of Amerigo Vespucci's letter. It was Waldseemüller who decided the newly discovered continent described by Vespucci should be called 'America' in his honour. Later he decided that Vespucci did not deserve the credit. He left out the name America on his next three maps, but it was too late, as he had already sold 1000 copies of the first version – so the name stuck.

Read all about it!

Before newspapers were produced, merchants and bankers who needed to know what was going on for their businesses paid for regular 'intelligencers' or 'courants', hand-written reports of the latest news from important cities.

Germany leads

The world's first newspaper was the *Relation*, published in Strasbourg in 1609, although a close rival is the German *Avisa Relation. The Leipziger Journal,* launched as a weekly in 1660, soon became the world's first daily newspaper. The *Wiener Zeitung,* first published in Vienna in 1703, is the oldest newspaper still being printed.

A 1643 issue of a weekly paper published in London carries news of the Civil War.

England catches up

In the 1620s Dutch printers began to send over to England 'corantos', cheaply-printed pamphlets of foreign news. During Britain's civil wars (1642–9), government control of printing broke down. Thousands of pamphlets were printed, all putting forward different political and religious points of view. By the late 1600s printed news-sheets were being circulated regularly in the London coffee houses, where men met for business. Their most important news was about ships' cargoes. London's first regular daily newspaper was the *Daily Courant,* published 1702–35. Newspapers soon appeared in **provincial** cities including Norwich, Bristol, Worcester and Exeter. By 1760 there were four London dailies; by 1790 there were fourteen. The number of provincial papers, usually published weekly, rose from 35 in 1760 to 150 by 1821.

The London Malignants disarmed, (89)
Fifty thousand pounds to be raised,
The Lord Capels Forces dispersed,
The Cavaliers from Glocester repulsed.

Numb. 12

Mercurius Civicus.
LONDONS
INTELLIGENCER:
OR,
Truth impartially related from thence to the whole Kingdome, to prevent mif-information.

From *Friday August* 11. to *Thursday August* 17. 1643.

Oth Houfes of Parliament and the City of *London*, have a long time been much indangered through the Plots and confpiracies of many malignant Inhabitants in that City, the Suburbs, and parts adjacent; notwithftanding which, that City, which in many other things of great confequence to this Nation both in former and latter time, hath afforded

M

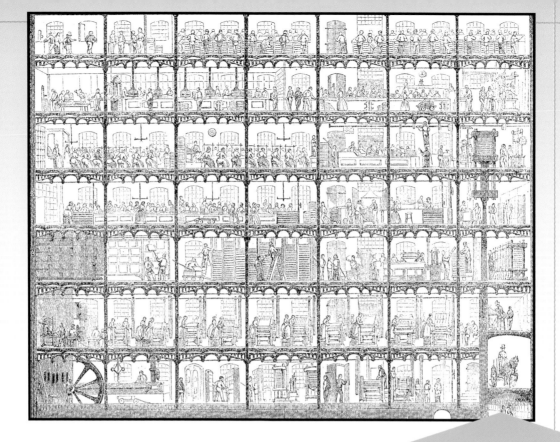

America

The American colonies' earliest newspaper, *Publick Occurrences*, appeared in 1690 and was banned by the government after one issue! In 1704, Scottish printer John Campbell began publishing a weekly *Boston News-Letter*. He took two-thirds of its contents from London papers, filling the rest with shipping news, law-court proceedings, extracts from sermons and brief notices about storms, deaths or other dramatic events.

Power of the press

By the nineteenth century, governments were increasingly chosen by voters rather than rulers. Newspaper reports of speeches and debates became an important link between politicians and voters. Newspapers' **editorial** columns and letters pages gave politicians feedback from public opinion about events and policies. Many political parties linked themselves with particular newspapers. Newspapers also investigated **scandals** and injustices, which the public then expected governments to remedy.

By the 19th century, newspapers were joined by magazines. This illustration from *Harper's New Monthly Magazine* shows how it was produced in New York in 1865. Notice the many women working there.

Prominent printers

Before the 20th century, printing was the main form of communication. Many famous printers were very successful and became rich and powerful.

Inventor

Boston-born Benjamin Franklin (1706–90) invented the lightning-conductor, bifocal lenses and a stove. He also helped to write America's Declaration of Independence and Constitution. But before all those achievements, he was a printer. In 1724–6 Franklin worked in London, the greatest centre for printing in the English-speaking world. Returning to America he won the contract to print paper money for Pennsylvania. He later printed official documents for New Jersey, Maryland and Delaware as well.

In 1729 he started a newspaper, the *Pennsylvania Gazette*. Between 1732 and 1758 he published each year an edition of *Poor Richard's Almanack*, a practical encyclopaedia containing **astronomical** information and farming notes, mixed in with verses and jokes. Franklin also set up Philadelphia's first library and an academy which became the University of Pennsylvania.

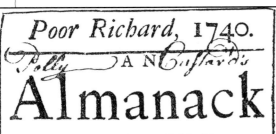

Poor Richard, 1740.

AN Saunders's

Polly

Almanack

For the Year of Christ

1740,

Being LEAP YEAR.

And makes since the Creation	Years.
By the Account of the Eastern *Greeks*	7248
By the Latin Church, when ☉ ent. ♈	6939
By the Computation of *W. W.*	5749
By the *Roman* Chronology	5689
By the *Jewish* Rabbies	5501

Wherein is contained,

The Lunations, Eclipses, Judgment of the Weather, Spring Tides, Planets Motions & mutual Aspects, Sun and Moon's Rising and Setting, Length of Days, Time of High Water, Fairs, Courts, and observable Days.

Fitted to the Latitude of Forty Degrees, and a Meridian of Five Hours West from *London*, but may without sensible Error, serve all the adjacent Places, even from *Newfoundland* to *South-Carolina*.

By *RICHARD SAUNDERS*, Philom.

PHILADELPHIA:
Printed and sold by *B. FRANKLIN*, at the New Printing-Office near the Market.

Benjamin Franklin's *Poor Richard's Almanack* became the only other book besides the Bible in many colonial American homes.

Writer

Samuel Richardson (1689–1761) had a business just off Fleet Street, the centre of London's printing trade. He produced books, magazines, advertising posters, letterheads and business cards. In 1723 he took over printing a political newspaper, the *True Briton* and in 1733 began printing for the House of Commons. In 1739–40 he wrote and published a novel, *Pamela,* which was widely praised. In France it was made into a play. Another novel, *Clarissa,* was translated into French, Dutch and German. In 1754–5 Richardson served as Master of the **Stationers' Company** – in effect the head of the printing profession.

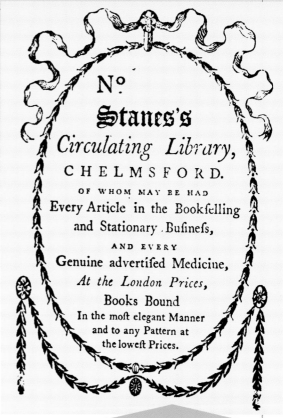

This enterprising 18th century English printer sold stationery and medicines, as well as typesetting, binding and lending out books.

Family businesses

Luke Hansard (1752–1828) took on responsibility for printing for the House of Commons when he was only 22 and this became the family business. His son Thomas (1776–1833) wrote a history and handbook of printing. The reports of House of Commons debates became known simply as *Hansard* and are still called this today.

Thomas De La Rue (1793–1866) began by making ladies' summer bonnets out of paper and went on to print headed stationery, playing cards, cheques and stamps. Warren De La Rue (1815–89) invented an envelope-making machine and in his leisure time pioneered astronomical photography. Sir Thomas De La Rue (1849–1911) made the firm a world-wide business, printing stamps and banknotes for many foreign countries.

The rise of the writer

Benjamin Franklin and Samuel Richardson were businessmen first and writers second. As more people learned to read and write, and had spare time to read for pleasure, it became possible to make a full-time living just from writing.

Fame...

Alice in Wonderland was originally written in a diary, with pictures by the author, Lewis Carroll.

Samuel Johnson (1709–84) lived in poverty for years before compiling the first true dictionary of the English language (1755), which made him famous. A generation later the English poets Shelley (1792–1822), Keats (1795–1821) and Byron (1788–1824) all found lasting fame, despite dying young. Novelist Jane Austen (1775–1817) was praised by Sir Walter Scott (1771–1832), the best-selling writer of his day, but lived a quiet country life. Jane Austen's novels are still widely read and have been adapted into TV dramas and films.

The *American Spelling Book* published in 1783 by Noah Webster (1758–1843), creator of the first dictionary of American English, sold about 100,000,000 copies over the following century. William Holmes McGuffey's 'readers', compiled from 1853 onwards to teach reading to Americans, sold over 125 million copies.

...and fortune

Writing novels raised Charles Dickens (1812–70) and W. M. Thackeray (1811–63) to fame and fortune. Anthony Trollope (1815–82) worked as a Post Office official and, writing from 5.30 until breakfast each morning before he went to work, produced 47 books to raise extra money to support his family. Washington Irving (1783–1859), creator of 'Rip Van Winkle', was the first American writer to become famous outside America. Mark Twain (1835–1910) – printer, river-boat pilot, gold-miner, editor – drew on his American adventures in humorous novels which made him popular on both sides of the Atlantic. Best-selling authors of the 20th century include American child-care expert Dr Benjamin Spock and English mystery author Agatha Christie.

American author, Mark Twain, on the day he received an honorary degree from Oxford University.

FOR YOUNGER READERS

Some of the world's best-selling books have been written mainly for younger readers. They include Lewis Carroll's *Alice in Wonderland* (1865) and Beatrix Potter's *The Tale of Peter Rabbit* (1902). Enid Blyton (1897–1968), creator of 'Noddy' and 'The Famous Five', wrote over 700 books, which have sold over 100 million copies in 1000 translations. Other best-selling children's authors of the century have included the creators of *The Cat in the Hat* (Dr Seuss – American), Tintin (Hergé – Belgian) and Asterix (René Goscinny – French).

Prints, posters, packaging

Profitable prints

English artist William Hogarth (1697–1764) trained as an **engraver.** He wanted to be a painter but knew that paintings often took a long time to complete and even longer to sell. Hogarth became successful by painting scenes of London life and then turning them into engravings. Instead of selling one expensive picture to one buyer, he could sell hundreds of cheap printed copies to many buyers. In 1735 he persuaded Parliament to pass a law giving artists **copyright** in their pictures, just like authors had with their books.

Publishers found a good market for books of prints showing beautiful natural views, the homes of the wealthy and scenes of foreign travel.
Around 1800 the English cartoonists Gillray, Rowlandson and Cruikshank produced hundreds of **caricatures** attacking the politicians and fashionable leaders of society.

CASTLE ACRE MONASTERY, in NORFOLK.

Prints of ruins were in demand, as picturesque views were very fashionable and popular.

Print for profits

As populations, incomes and **literacy** all expanded rapidly in the 19th century, huge printing opportunities opened up to supply the needs of businesses for headed bills, receipts, **ledgers** and labels. The increased use of paper money produced a need for banknotes that were difficult to **forge.** Railways, steamship and bus companies needed tickets. More and more foodstuffs and medicines were sold in sealed packets, which carried printed information or advertising. In 1840 Britain issued the world's first pre-paid sticky postage stamps. Other countries quickly copied the idea. From the 1880s onwards there was a need for telephone directories. Specialized businesses emerged producing, for example, tickets numbered in sequence or invitation cards printed in gold.

POSTERS, POLITICS AND PLEASURE

The first posters were government announcements of new laws, taxes or chances to join the army. As more people could read and vote, political parties began to use posters to get support at elections. Theatres used posters to tell audiences about their changing programmes. In France clubs, restaurants, exhibitions and galleries employed artists to design pictorial posters to attract customers. Posters by artists such as Jules Chéret (1836–1932), Henri Toulouse-Lautrec (1864–1901) or Alphonse Mucha (1860–1939) are now regarded as important works of art.

THE MANAGERS OF THE NEW

IPSWICH THEATRE,

Beg most respectfully to inform their Patrons and the public in general, that they have, at a very considerable outlay, completed their arrangements, and having also engaged some of the best Vocal Performers, in addition to their Establishment, intend opening their Theatre on the 31st inst., with the popular Comedy of

WHIG GRATITUDE :

OR,

A NEW WAY TO PAY OLD DEBTS.

In which the celebrated Performers will introduce the following New Songs, written entirely for the occasion, and of which the Managers have the entire Copyright.

BILLY BLOATER,

ALIAS,

THE MITY MAN.

"Did I not Soap the knowing ones."
"Could I refuse, when he married my sisters."
"I'm badly off, for Tin, my friend."

SHUFFLING JOHNNY.

"Oh Give me, Give me, Burton Ale."
"I've Butter, Cheese, and Lard in Store."

Allen Broadbrim

"The Renegade."
"Can I not tell a dirty tale."

JERRY SMOOTHFACE.

"I'd golden Hopes in Railway Shares,
Alas! they now are gone."

HOOKEY GEORGE.

"We are all in the Hadleigh Line."

TOMMY DYE.

"My Mother would not give consent."

Messrs. Gaslight & Glyster

Will also introduce the pathetic Duet of
"Farewell to the Ward of St. Clement for ever."

To conclude with the celebrated Hornpipe called the

JACKALL's JIG

By LOTTO HENSERO

One of the Black Monkey tribe, who will be exhibited for a few nights only, as his Proprietor has determined to travel with him in a Puppet-show, with a collection of other animals of a similar nature.

The Managers beg also to state that they have another Play in Rehearsal, called

THE THIMBLE-RIG COMPANY.

The particulars of which will be printed in a few days.

Ipswich: Smith, Brown, Jones, Robinson, Printers to the Establishment.

Cheap posters using many different **typefaces** brought regular income to **provincial** printers.

Better and better, faster and faster

How printing spread

There were printers in over 100 European cities and towns by 1480, and in over 230 by 1500. By then, around a thousand printing presses had produced several million books. During the 16th century, Germany produced 45,000 different titles, France 38,000 and England 10,000. Italy and the Netherlands also had important printing industries. This opened up the world to people who, before that, had known little beyond their own town or village. The rapid spread of new ideas, particularly about religion and politics, changed Europe's history for ever.

New print

The earliest printed books were made to look as much like traditional hand-copied books as possible. As printed books became more popular, though, printers designed new **typefaces** especially for printing. Two of the most famous are Roman (1470) and Italic (1501). These were far easier to read than the earliest kind of print, which imitated handwriting.

The Stanhope press, invented in 1800, could print much bigger sheets than earlier presses, much more quickly.

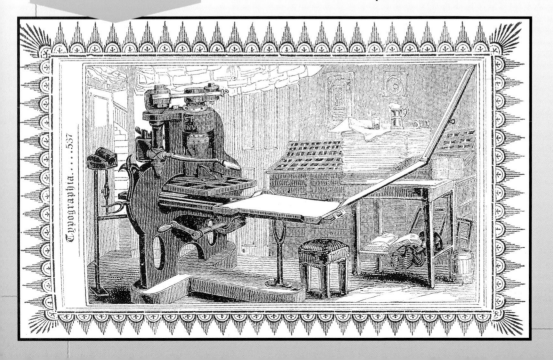

Faster

In Gutenberg's day a hard-working printer could turn out perhaps 300 pages a day because he had to open the press to insert each sheet of blank paper. In 1620 Dutch printer Willem Blaeu introduced a **counter-weighted** press, which opened automatically as each sheet was printed. A printer could now run off 150 copies an hour.

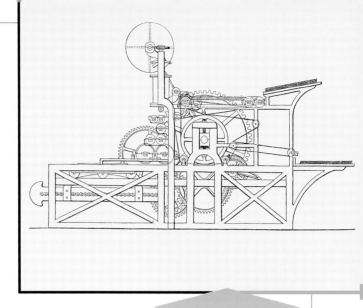

A drawing of a steam-powered Koenig press; no actual examples have survived.

Shade and colour

Early printers could not make gradual tones, shading from black through grey to white. But in 1642 Colonel Ludwig von Siegen of Hesse in Germany invented a method using copper plates, roughened to hold printing ink, but smoothed and cleaned of ink for a white or grey effect. This process, called 'mezzotint' from the Italian for 'half-tint', can show fine differences of light and shade. It was used for printing portraits and works of art. Full-colour printing, mixing red, yellow and blue inks to produce a wide range of colours, was also developed in Germany in 1719.

Faster presses

In 1800 the English Lord Stanhope invented a printing press made of iron, not wood. This could print much bigger sheets at a rate of 250 an hour. Between 1810 and 1816 Friedrich Koenig (1774–1833), a German working in London, perfected a steam-powered printing press which could print both sides of a sheet at once at a rate of 1100 an hour. By 1848 rotary presses, printing from a circular drum, not a flat sheet of **type,** could turn out 8000 copies an hour.

Back to beautiful books

The use of steam-powered machinery to print books on paper made from wood pulp, and to bind them in cotton or cardboard covers, meant that more people could afford them. The books themselves, however, were not lovely to look at or handle. Cheap ink faded. Cheap paper cracked. Cheap bindings and covers were easily torn or fell apart.

Crusade for beauty

When he was in his 50s, English artist and poet William Morris (1834–96) decided to revive the art of making fine books. He was already rich enough to finance his hobby, as well as being qualified for the task. Morris was famous for designing wallpapers and textiles. He was also a superb **calligrapher**, an expert on English literature and had a fine collection of old books and manuscripts. Morris had strong views about art and work. He believed beautiful things would only be produced by craftsmen who enjoyed their work and took pride in it.

This Kelmscott Chaucer is on display at William Morris's childhood home, Water House, at Walthamstow, East London.

Morris founded the Kelmscott Press in 1891 in his house at Hammersmith, London, and printed 52 different titles. His greatest achievement was an edition of Chaucer's *Canterbury Tales*. Morris himself designed the **typeface**, based on 15th century writing styles. His friend, the artist Edward Burne-Jones, did the illustrations. Each page was meant to be as pleasing as a picture.

Private presses

The Kelmscott Press inspired the founding of other private printing presses on both sides of the Atlantic. Their aim was not to make money but to present the best of literature in the best possible way. C. R. Ashbee, a follower of Morris, took over his printing press to found Essex House Press (1898–1910) in London's East End. Charles Ricketts' Vale Press (1896–1903) printed all of Shakespeare's works in 39 volumes. French artist Lucien Pissarro took over the Vale Press **types** for his Eragny Press, which introduced elegant patterned paper bindings. The Doves Press (1901–20) produced a splendid five-volume Bible for use in churches.

20TH CENTURY PRINTERS AND TYPOGRAPHERS

America's greatest book designer, Bruce Rogers (1870–1957) created the Centaur typeface used by the Metropolitan Museum of Art, and he also worked with Harvard University Press. D. B. Updike (1860–1941), a follower of Morris, founded the Merrymount Press and taught printing history at Harvard. In San Francisco Edwin and Robert Grabhorn printed books for the Book Club of California. English **engraver**, Eric Gill (1882-1940) is probably best remembered as the designer of the typeface known as Gill Sans serif.

This is a sentence written in

CENTAUR TYPE FACE

designed by Bruce Rogers in 1915.

Pages without printing

Invention by accident

In 1904 New York printer Ira Rubel noticed by chance that a rubber pad could transfer the image from an inked metal printing plate onto paper – and make a better picture than the actual plate could. This led to the process of offset printing by which the image or text is transferred – offset – from a zinc printing plate to a rubber-covered cylinder and then rolled onto paper. This process is faster and cheaper than any earlier methods. Modern offset machines can print 70,000 newspapers an hour, using reels holding up to 20 kilometres of paper.

Invention by design

Setting **type** into page-size 'formes' or frames was a skilled craft. The **compositor** used a keyboard like a typewriter to set lines of type for a metal mould. Then in 1939 American William Heubner invented a process called photosetting, using a machine that projected characters onto film at the tap of a key. By 1954, improved photosetting machines could set 1000 characters a minute. In 1957 English publisher Penguin photoset a book for the first time.

Typesetters at work in a newspaper office around 1900 – the work was skilled, clean and well paid.

Electronic publishing

In 1947 the American Fairchild Corporation developed an electronic scanner, which beamed a picture onto a spinning drum. Signals were sent to a cutter that engraved a copy of the image on the printing surface. Computer-controlled systems were developed in Germany in the 1960s. In 1982 the Postscript software language enabled printers to make up pages of text and pictures electronically. In 1985 Pagemaker software adapted the process for personal computers.

Authors abandoned typewriters to deliver books on disk. By the 1990s journalists equipped with a laptop, digital camera and cellphone could use satellite communications to beam words and images from anywhere in the world straight to their home newsdesk and into the newspaper's mainframe computer. Nowadays newspapers and books are sent by electronic pulses between computer terminals before the presses finally roll and print them on paper.

In March 2000, best selling author, Stephen King, published a short story straight onto the internet. Readers paid $2 to download it, bypassing the printing process altogether. Is this another turning point for printing?

Modern page-layout is done with specialist computer programs such as QuarkXpress, which runs on Apple Mac and PC computers.

Time-line

105	Paper known to be in use in China
698–700	*Lindisfarne Gospel* copied by Bishop Eadfrith
795	Paper-making known in Baghdad, Iraq
983	Chinese print complete Buddhist scriptures
1086	*Domesday Book* compiled in England
1455	*Gutenberg Bible* printed
1468	Death of Johannes Gutenberg
1476	William Caxton brings printing to England
1501	Italic typeface introduced
1507	Waldseemüller names America
1522	Luther translates New Testament from Greek and Hebrew into German
1525	William Tyndale's English translation of the New Testament is printed in Cologne
1534	Luther translates entire Bible into German
1554	Foxe's *Book of Martyrs* published
1588	Bible printed in Welsh
1609	World's first newspaper published in Strasbourg
1615	*Frankfurter Journal* published
1620	Blaeu's counter-weighted press introduced
1642	Mezzotint process invented
1702	*Daily Courant,* London's first regular daily newspaper, published
1703	*Wiener Zeitung* published in Vienna, and still being printed
1704	*Boston Newsletter* published in America
1719	Full-colour printing pioneered in Germany
1733	Benjamin Franklin begins publishing *Poor Richard's Almanack*
1735	Hogarth persuades Parliament to pass Copyright Act
1755	Samuel Johnson's *Dictionary* completed
1774	Luke Hansard prints the debates of the British House of Commons
1783	Noah Webster publishes *American Spelling Book*
1799	Machine for making paper as a roll, not sheets, invented in France
1816	Koenig steam-powered rotary press perfected
1840	Penny Black postage stamp issued in Britain
1848	Rotary presses produce 8000 copies per hour
1891	William Morris founds the Kelmscott Press
1904	Ira Rubel pioneers offset printing
1939	William Heubner pioneers photo-typesetting
1982	Electronic page-making introduced
2000	Stephen King publishes short story straight onto internet

Glossary

alloy	mixture of metals
antimony	poisonous, silvery white metal used in casting type
astronomical	relating to the science of the movements of stars and planets
calligraphy	the art of beautiful writing
caricature	cartoon exaggerating faces and features
cast	make an object by pouring hot metal into a mould
charter	legal document granting right to hold land or market
chronicle	official record of important events
compositor	person who composes type into pages ready for printing
copyright	legal ownership of the right to reproduce a book or work of art
counter-weight	weight suspended near the end of a moving part of a machine that makes it easier to work the machine
editorial	the parts of a newspaper written by the people who run it, giving their opinions on the news
engraver	someone who carves designs into printing plates
forge	to make an illegal copy of something valuable, such as a banknote
heresy	having beliefs that do not agree with those of the Church
ledger	large book for keeping accounts of money earned and paid out
literate	able to read and write
logbook	official record of a voyage kept by the captain of a ship
monastery	community of monks
parchment	fine writing surface made by scraping and cleaning animal skin
provincial	relating to the areas other than the capital city of a country
quill	pen made from a bird's feather cut to a point
scandals	events which most people would believe to be wrong
scribe	person who makes a living by copying out documents or writing letters for others
scriptorium	writing-room of a monastery, usually sited to catch bright light from the north
scriptures	sacred writings of a religion
sermon	talk given by a church leader and based on the Bible, to explain how Christians should behave
Stationers' Company	London-based organization founded in 1557 to control training and production in the printing trade; its powers could be used to suppress books government disapproved of
treaty	formal agreement, often between two countries
type	small block of metal cast in relief to bear a letter or mark used in printing
typeface	set of type made to a particular style or size
typography	the study of typefaces

Index